50 Cookies Made in the Oven Dishes

By: Kelly Johnson

Table of Contents

- Chocolate Chip Cookies
- Snickerdoodles
- Peanut Butter Cookies
- Oatmeal Raisin Cookies
- Sugar Cookies
- Gingerbread Cookies
- White Chocolate Macadamia Nut Cookies
- Shortbread Cookies
- Lemon Sugar Cookies
- Molasses Cookies
- Double Chocolate Chip Cookies
- Almond Cookies
- Coconut Macaroons
- Chocolate Crinkle Cookies
- Butter Pecan Cookies
- Pumpkin Spice Cookies
- M&M Cookies
- Salted Caramel Cookies
- Trail Mix Cookies
- Red Velvet Cookies
- Hazelnut Chocolate Chip Cookies
- Brownie Cookies
- Cinnamon Roll Cookies
- Cherry Almond Cookies
- Apricot Jam Thumbprint Cookies
- Oatmeal Chocolate Chip Cookies
- S'mores Cookies
- Toffee Pecan Cookies
- Matcha Green Tea Cookies
- Coffee Chocolate Chip Cookies
- Raspberry Coconut Cookies
- Funfetti Cookies
- Double Peanut Butter Cookies
- Cashew Cookies
- Carrot Cake Cookies

- Chocolate Dipped Biscotti
- Poppy Seed Cookies
- Maple Pecan Cookies
- Nutella Stuffed Cookies
- Cranberry White Chocolate Cookies
- Chai Spice Cookies
- Banana Bread Cookies
- Pistachio Cookies
- Chocolate Mint Cookies
- Apple Cinnamon Cookies
- Chocolate Fudge Cookies
- Cocoa Nib Cookies
- Lemon Poppy Seed Cookies
- Cinnamon Sugar Cookies
- Rocky Road Cookies

Chocolate Chip Cookies

Ingredients:

- 1 cup butter, softened
- 3/4 cup brown sugar
- 1/4 cup white sugar
- 2 tsp vanilla extract
- 2 large eggs
- 2 1/4 cups all-purpose flour
- 1 tsp baking soda
- 1/2 tsp salt
- 2 cups semi-sweet chocolate chips

Instructions:

1. Preheat oven to 350°F (175°C).
2. Cream together butter, brown sugar, and white sugar until fluffy.
3. Add vanilla and eggs, mixing well.
4. In another bowl, combine flour, baking soda, and salt, then gradually add to the wet ingredients.
5. Stir in chocolate chips.
6. Drop spoonfuls of dough onto a baking sheet and bake for 10-12 minutes.

Snickerdoodles

Ingredients:

- 1 cup butter, softened
- 1 1/2 cups sugar
- 2 large eggs
- 2 3/4 cups all-purpose flour
- 2 tsp cream of tartar
- 1 tsp baking soda
- 1/2 tsp salt
- 2 tbsp sugar (for rolling)
- 2 tsp cinnamon (for rolling)

Instructions:

1. Preheat oven to 350°F (175°C).
2. Cream together butter and sugar.
3. Add eggs and mix until smooth.
4. In a separate bowl, mix flour, cream of tartar, baking soda, and salt.
5. Gradually combine with the wet ingredients.
6. In a small bowl, mix 2 tbsp sugar and cinnamon. Roll dough into balls and coat in cinnamon sugar.
7. Bake for 8-10 minutes.

Peanut Butter Cookies

Ingredients:

- 1 cup peanut butter
- 1 cup sugar
- 1 large egg
- 1 tsp vanilla extract

Instructions:

1. Preheat oven to 350°F (175°C).
2. Mix together peanut butter, sugar, egg, and vanilla until smooth.
3. Drop dough by spoonfuls onto a baking sheet.
4. Use a fork to press down and create a criss-cross pattern on top of each cookie.
5. Bake for 8-10 minutes.

Oatmeal Raisin Cookies

Ingredients:

- 1 cup butter, softened
- 1 cup brown sugar
- 1/2 cup white sugar
- 2 large eggs
- 1 tsp vanilla extract
- 1 1/2 cups all-purpose flour
- 1 tsp baking soda
- 1/2 tsp salt
- 1 1/2 cups rolled oats
- 1 cup raisins

Instructions:

1. Preheat oven to 350°F (175°C).
2. Cream together butter, brown sugar, and white sugar.
3. Add eggs and vanilla, mixing well.
4. In another bowl, combine flour, baking soda, and salt.
5. Stir in oats and raisins.
6. Drop dough by spoonfuls onto a baking sheet.
7. Bake for 10-12 minutes.

Sugar Cookies

Ingredients:

- 1 cup butter, softened
- 1 1/2 cups sugar
- 1 large egg
- 1 1/2 tsp vanilla extract
- 2 3/4 cups all-purpose flour
- 1 tsp baking soda
- 1/2 tsp salt

Instructions:

1. Preheat oven to 350°F (175°C).
2. Cream together butter and sugar.
3. Add egg and vanilla, mixing until smooth.
4. In a separate bowl, combine flour, baking soda, and salt.
5. Gradually add dry ingredients to wet ingredients.
6. Roll dough into balls and flatten with a glass.
7. Bake for 8-10 minutes.

Gingerbread Cookies

Ingredients:

- 3 1/4 cups all-purpose flour
- 1 tsp baking soda
- 1 tsp ground cinnamon
- 1 tsp ground ginger
- 1/2 tsp ground cloves
- 1/4 tsp salt
- 1/2 cup butter, softened
- 1/2 cup brown sugar
- 1 large egg
- 1/2 cup molasses

Instructions:

1. Preheat oven to 350°F (175°C).
2. In a bowl, combine flour, baking soda, cinnamon, ginger, cloves, and salt.
3. In another bowl, cream butter and brown sugar. Add egg and molasses.
4. Gradually add dry ingredients to the wet mixture and mix until combined.
5. Roll dough out and cut into shapes.
6. Bake for 8-10 minutes.

White Chocolate Macadamia Nut Cookies

Ingredients:

- 1 cup butter, softened
- 3/4 cup brown sugar
- 1/2 cup white sugar
- 2 large eggs
- 1 tsp vanilla extract
- 2 1/2 cups all-purpose flour
- 1 tsp baking soda
- 1/2 tsp salt
- 1 cup white chocolate chips
- 1 cup macadamia nuts, chopped

Instructions:

1. Preheat oven to 350°F (175°C).
2. Cream together butter, brown sugar, and white sugar.
3. Add eggs and vanilla, mixing well.
4. In a separate bowl, combine flour, baking soda, and salt.
5. Stir in white chocolate chips and macadamia nuts.
6. Drop dough by spoonfuls onto a baking sheet.
7. Bake for 10-12 minutes.

Shortbread Cookies

Ingredients:

- 1 cup butter, softened
- 1/2 cup sugar
- 2 cups all-purpose flour
- 1/4 tsp salt

Instructions:

1. Preheat oven to 350°F (175°C).
2. Cream together butter and sugar.
3. Gradually add flour and salt, mixing until dough forms.
4. Roll dough out and cut into shapes.
5. Bake for 12-15 minutes until lightly golden.

Lemon Sugar Cookies

Ingredients:

- 1 cup butter, softened
- 1 1/2 cups sugar
- 1 large egg
- 1 tbsp lemon zest
- 1/4 tsp lemon juice
- 2 cups all-purpose flour
- 1 tsp baking soda
- 1/4 tsp salt

Instructions:

1. Preheat oven to 350°F (175°C).
2. Cream together butter and sugar.
3. Add egg, lemon zest, and lemon juice.
4. In a separate bowl, combine flour, baking soda, and salt.
5. Gradually add dry ingredients to wet ingredients.
6. Roll dough into balls and flatten with a glass.
7. Bake for 8-10 minutes.

Molasses Cookies

Ingredients:

- 1 cup butter, softened
- 1 cup brown sugar
- 1/4 cup molasses
- 1 large egg
- 2 1/4 cups all-purpose flour
- 2 tsp baking soda
- 1 tsp ground cinnamon
- 1 tsp ground ginger
- 1/2 tsp ground cloves
- 1/4 tsp salt

Instructions:

1. Preheat oven to 350°F (175°C).
2. Cream together butter, brown sugar, and molasses.
3. Add egg and mix until smooth.
4. In another bowl, combine flour, baking soda, cinnamon, ginger, cloves, and salt.
5. Gradually add dry ingredients to wet ingredients.
6. Roll dough into balls and coat with sugar.
7. Bake for 8-10 minutes.

Double Chocolate Chip Cookies

Ingredients:

- 1 cup butter, softened
- 3/4 cup brown sugar
- 1/4 cup white sugar
- 2 large eggs
- 1 tsp vanilla extract
- 1 3/4 cups all-purpose flour
- 1/2 cup cocoa powder
- 1 tsp baking soda
- 1/4 tsp salt
- 1 1/2 cups semi-sweet chocolate chips

Instructions:

1. Preheat oven to 350°F (175°C).
2. Cream together butter, brown sugar, and white sugar.
3. Add eggs and vanilla, mixing well.
4. In another bowl, combine flour, cocoa powder, baking soda, and salt.
5. Gradually add dry ingredients to wet ingredients.
6. Stir in chocolate chips.
7. Drop dough by spoonfuls onto a baking sheet.
8. Bake for 10-12 minutes.

Almond Cookies

Ingredients:

- 1 cup butter, softened
- 1 cup sugar
- 1 large egg
- 1 tsp almond extract
- 2 cups all-purpose flour
- 1/2 tsp baking powder
- 1/4 tsp salt
- 1/2 cup sliced almonds

Instructions:

1. Preheat oven to 350°F (175°C).
2. Cream together butter and sugar until fluffy.
3. Add egg and almond extract, mixing well.
4. In a separate bowl, combine flour, baking powder, and salt. Gradually add to the wet mixture.
5. Stir in sliced almonds.
6. Drop dough by spoonfuls onto a baking sheet.
7. Bake for 10-12 minutes or until edges are lightly golden.

Coconut Macaroons

Ingredients:

- 2 1/2 cups sweetened shredded coconut
- 1/2 cup sugar
- 2 large egg whites
- 1 tsp vanilla extract
- 1/4 tsp salt

Instructions:

1. Preheat oven to 325°F (163°C).
2. In a bowl, combine coconut, sugar, egg whites, vanilla, and salt. Mix until well combined.
3. Drop rounded spoonfuls of the mixture onto a baking sheet lined with parchment paper.
4. Bake for 18-20 minutes or until golden brown.
5. Allow to cool completely before serving.

Chocolate Crinkle Cookies

Ingredients:

- 1 cup butter, softened
- 1 1/2 cups sugar
- 1 large egg
- 1 tsp vanilla extract
- 1/2 cup cocoa powder
- 2 cups all-purpose flour
- 2 tsp baking powder
- 1/4 tsp salt
- 1/2 cup powdered sugar

Instructions:

1. Preheat oven to 350°F (175°C).
2. Cream together butter and sugar until smooth.
3. Add egg and vanilla extract, mixing well.
4. In another bowl, combine cocoa powder, flour, baking powder, and salt. Gradually add to the wet mixture.
5. Roll dough into balls, then roll each ball in powdered sugar.
6. Place on a baking sheet and bake for 10-12 minutes.

Butter Pecan Cookies

Ingredients:

- 1 cup butter, softened
- 1 cup brown sugar
- 1 large egg
- 2 tsp vanilla extract
- 2 cups all-purpose flour
- 1 tsp baking soda
- 1/2 tsp salt
- 1 cup chopped pecans

Instructions:

1. Preheat oven to 350°F (175°C).
2. Cream together butter and brown sugar.
3. Add egg and vanilla, mixing well.
4. In another bowl, combine flour, baking soda, and salt. Gradually add to the wet ingredients.
5. Stir in chopped pecans.
6. Drop spoonfuls of dough onto a baking sheet.
7. Bake for 10-12 minutes or until golden brown.

Pumpkin Spice Cookies

Ingredients:

- 1 cup butter, softened
- 1 cup sugar
- 1 cup pumpkin puree
- 1 large egg
- 1 tsp vanilla extract
- 2 1/2 cups all-purpose flour
- 1 tsp baking soda
- 1/2 tsp salt
- 1 1/2 tsp ground cinnamon
- 1/2 tsp ground nutmeg
- 1/2 tsp ground ginger

Instructions:

1. Preheat oven to 350°F (175°C).
2. Cream together butter and sugar.
3. Add pumpkin puree, egg, and vanilla, mixing well.
4. In another bowl, combine flour, baking soda, salt, cinnamon, nutmeg, and ginger.
5. Gradually add dry ingredients to the wet mixture.
6. Drop dough by spoonfuls onto a baking sheet.
7. Bake for 12-15 minutes until lightly golden.

M&M Cookies

Ingredients:

- 1 cup butter, softened
- 3/4 cup brown sugar
- 1/4 cup white sugar
- 2 large eggs
- 1 tsp vanilla extract
- 2 1/4 cups all-purpose flour
- 1 tsp baking soda
- 1/2 tsp salt
- 1 1/2 cups M&M candies

Instructions:

1. Preheat oven to 350°F (175°C).
2. Cream together butter, brown sugar, and white sugar.
3. Add eggs and vanilla, mixing well.
4. In another bowl, combine flour, baking soda, and salt. Gradually add to the wet ingredients.
5. Stir in M&M candies.
6. Drop dough by spoonfuls onto a baking sheet.
7. Bake for 10-12 minutes.

Salted Caramel Cookies

Ingredients:

- 1 cup butter, softened
- 3/4 cup brown sugar
- 1/4 cup white sugar
- 1 large egg
- 2 tsp vanilla extract
- 2 cups all-purpose flour
- 1 tsp baking soda
- 1/2 tsp salt
- 1/2 cup caramel bits or caramel sauce
- 1 tsp sea salt

Instructions:

1. Preheat oven to 350°F (175°C).
2. Cream together butter, brown sugar, and white sugar.
3. Add egg and vanilla, mixing well.
4. In a separate bowl, combine flour, baking soda, and salt. Gradually add to the wet ingredients.
5. Stir in caramel bits or drizzle caramel sauce into dough.
6. Drop dough onto a baking sheet and sprinkle with sea salt.
7. Bake for 10-12 minutes.

Trail Mix Cookies

Ingredients:

- 1 cup butter, softened
- 3/4 cup brown sugar
- 1/4 cup white sugar
- 2 large eggs
- 1 tsp vanilla extract
- 2 cups all-purpose flour
- 1 tsp baking soda
- 1/2 tsp salt
- 1 cup trail mix (nuts, dried fruit, and chocolate chips)

Instructions:

1. Preheat oven to 350°F (175°C).
2. Cream together butter, brown sugar, and white sugar.
3. Add eggs and vanilla, mixing well.
4. In a separate bowl, combine flour, baking soda, and salt. Gradually add to the wet ingredients.
5. Stir in trail mix.
6. Drop dough onto a baking sheet.
7. Bake for 10-12 minutes.

Red Velvet Cookies

Ingredients:

- 1 cup butter, softened
- 1 cup sugar
- 1 large egg
- 2 tbsp red food coloring
- 1 tsp vanilla extract
- 2 1/4 cups all-purpose flour
- 1 tsp baking soda
- 1/2 tsp salt
- 2 tbsp cocoa powder
- 1/2 cup white chocolate chips

Instructions:

1. Preheat oven to 350°F (175°C).
2. Cream together butter and sugar.
3. Add egg, food coloring, and vanilla, mixing well.
4. In a separate bowl, combine flour, baking soda, salt, and cocoa powder. Gradually add to the wet ingredients.
5. Stir in white chocolate chips.
6. Drop dough onto a baking sheet and bake for 10-12 minutes.

Hazelnut Chocolate Chip Cookies

Ingredients:

- 1 cup butter, softened
- 3/4 cup brown sugar
- 1/4 cup white sugar
- 2 large eggs
- 1 tsp vanilla extract
- 2 cups all-purpose flour
- 1 tsp baking soda
- 1/2 tsp salt
- 1 cup chocolate chips
- 1 cup chopped hazelnuts

Instructions:

1. Preheat oven to 350°F (175°C).
2. Cream together butter, brown sugar, and white sugar.
3. Add eggs and vanilla, mixing well.
4. In another bowl, combine flour, baking soda, and salt. Gradually add to the wet ingredients.
5. Stir in chocolate chips and hazelnuts.
6. Drop dough onto a baking sheet.
7. Bake for 10-12 minutes.

Brownie Cookies

Ingredients:

- 1/2 cup butter, melted
- 1 cup sugar
- 1 large egg
- 1 tsp vanilla extract
- 1/2 cup all-purpose flour
- 1/2 cup unsweetened cocoa powder
- 1/4 tsp baking powder
- 1/4 tsp salt
- 1/2 cup chocolate chips

Instructions:

1. Preheat oven to 350°F (175°C).
2. In a bowl, combine melted butter and sugar.
3. Add egg and vanilla extract, mixing well.
4. In a separate bowl, whisk together flour, cocoa powder, baking powder, and salt. Gradually add to the wet ingredients.
5. Stir in chocolate chips.
6. Drop spoonfuls of dough onto a baking sheet.
7. Bake for 10-12 minutes or until set.

Cinnamon Roll Cookies

Ingredients:

- 1 cup butter, softened
- 1 cup sugar
- 1 large egg
- 1 tsp vanilla extract
- 2 1/2 cups all-purpose flour
- 1/2 tsp baking powder
- 1/4 tsp salt
- 1 tbsp ground cinnamon
- 1/2 cup brown sugar

Instructions:

1. Preheat oven to 350°F (175°C).
2. Cream together butter and sugar until fluffy.
3. Add egg and vanilla extract, mixing well.
4. In a separate bowl, combine flour, baking powder, and salt. Gradually add to the wet mixture.
5. Mix cinnamon and brown sugar together. Roll dough into a log and sprinkle the cinnamon-sugar mixture on top. Roll it up and chill for 30 minutes.
6. Slice dough into rounds and place on a baking sheet.
7. Bake for 10-12 minutes.

Cherry Almond Cookies

Ingredients:

- 1 cup butter, softened
- 1 cup sugar
- 1 large egg
- 1 tsp almond extract
- 2 1/2 cups all-purpose flour
- 1 tsp baking soda
- 1/4 tsp salt
- 1/2 cup chopped dried cherries
- 1/2 cup sliced almonds

Instructions:

1. Preheat oven to 350°F (175°C).
2. Cream together butter and sugar.
3. Add egg and almond extract, mixing well.
4. In a separate bowl, combine flour, baking soda, and salt. Gradually add to the wet mixture.
5. Stir in dried cherries and almonds.
6. Drop dough by spoonfuls onto a baking sheet.
7. Bake for 10-12 minutes.

Apricot Jam Thumbprint Cookies

Ingredients:

- 1 cup butter, softened
- 1/2 cup sugar
- 1 large egg
- 1 tsp vanilla extract
- 2 cups all-purpose flour
- 1/2 tsp baking powder
- 1/4 tsp salt
- 1/4 cup apricot jam

Instructions:

1. Preheat oven to 350°F (175°C).
2. Cream together butter and sugar until light and fluffy.
3. Add egg and vanilla extract, mixing well.
4. In a separate bowl, combine flour, baking powder, and salt. Gradually add to the wet mixture.
5. Roll dough into balls and place on a baking sheet.
6. Press your thumb into the center of each cookie to make an indent.
7. Fill the indent with apricot jam.
8. Bake for 10-12 minutes.

Oatmeal Chocolate Chip Cookies

Ingredients:

- 1 cup butter, softened
- 3/4 cup brown sugar
- 1/4 cup white sugar
- 2 large eggs
- 1 tsp vanilla extract
- 1 1/2 cups rolled oats
- 1 cup all-purpose flour
- 1 tsp baking soda
- 1/2 tsp salt
- 1 cup chocolate chips

Instructions:

1. Preheat oven to 350°F (175°C).
2. Cream together butter, brown sugar, and white sugar.
3. Add eggs and vanilla, mixing well.
4. In another bowl, combine oats, flour, baking soda, and salt. Gradually add to the wet mixture.
5. Stir in chocolate chips.
6. Drop dough onto a baking sheet.
7. Bake for 10-12 minutes.

S'mores Cookies

Ingredients:

- 1 cup butter, softened
- 1 cup sugar
- 1 large egg
- 1 tsp vanilla extract
- 2 cups all-purpose flour
- 1/2 tsp baking soda
- 1/4 tsp salt
- 1 cup chocolate chips
- 1 cup mini marshmallows
- 1 cup graham cracker crumbs

Instructions:

1. Preheat oven to 350°F (175°C).
2. Cream together butter and sugar until fluffy.
3. Add egg and vanilla extract, mixing well.
4. In another bowl, combine flour, baking soda, and salt. Gradually add to the wet mixture.
5. Stir in chocolate chips, marshmallows, and graham cracker crumbs.
6. Drop dough by spoonfuls onto a baking sheet.
7. Bake for 10-12 minutes.

Toffee Pecan Cookies

Ingredients:

- 1 cup butter, softened
- 3/4 cup brown sugar
- 1/4 cup white sugar
- 2 large eggs
- 1 tsp vanilla extract
- 2 cups all-purpose flour
- 1 tsp baking soda
- 1/2 tsp salt
- 1 cup toffee bits
- 1 cup chopped pecans

Instructions:

1. Preheat oven to 350°F (175°C).
2. Cream together butter, brown sugar, and white sugar.
3. Add eggs and vanilla, mixing well.
4. In a separate bowl, combine flour, baking soda, and salt. Gradually add to the wet mixture.
5. Stir in toffee bits and pecans.
6. Drop dough onto a baking sheet.
7. Bake for 10-12 minutes.

Matcha Green Tea Cookies

Ingredients:

- 1 cup butter, softened
- 3/4 cup sugar
- 1 large egg
- 2 tbsp matcha green tea powder
- 2 cups all-purpose flour
- 1 tsp baking soda
- 1/4 tsp salt

Instructions:

1. Preheat oven to 350°F (175°C).
2. Cream together butter and sugar.
3. Add egg and matcha powder, mixing well.
4. In another bowl, combine flour, baking soda, and salt. Gradually add to the wet mixture.
5. Drop dough by spoonfuls onto a baking sheet.
6. Bake for 10-12 minutes.

Coffee Chocolate Chip Cookies

Ingredients:

- 1 cup butter, softened
- 3/4 cup brown sugar
- 1/4 cup white sugar
- 2 large eggs
- 1 tsp vanilla extract
- 1 1/2 cups all-purpose flour
- 1 tsp baking soda
- 1/2 tsp salt
- 1 tbsp instant coffee granules
- 1 cup chocolate chips

Instructions:

1. Preheat oven to 350°F (175°C).
2. Cream together butter, brown sugar, and white sugar.
3. Add eggs and vanilla, mixing well.
4. In a separate bowl, combine flour, baking soda, salt, and instant coffee. Gradually add to the wet mixture.
5. Stir in chocolate chips.
6. Drop dough onto a baking sheet.
7. Bake for 10-12 minutes.

Raspberry Coconut Cookies

Ingredients:

- 1 cup butter, softened
- 1 cup sugar
- 1 large egg
- 1 tsp vanilla extract
- 1 cup shredded coconut
- 2 cups all-purpose flour
- 1/2 tsp baking soda
- 1/4 tsp salt
- 1/2 cup fresh raspberries

Instructions:

1. Preheat oven to 350°F (175°C).
2. Cream together butter and sugar.
3. Add egg and vanilla, mixing well.
4. In a separate bowl, combine coconut, flour, baking soda, and salt. Gradually add to the wet mixture.
5. Gently fold in raspberries.
6. Drop dough by spoonfuls onto a baking sheet.
7. Bake for 10-12 minutes.

Funfetti Cookies

Ingredients:

- 1 cup butter, softened
- 3/4 cup sugar
- 1/4 cup brown sugar
- 1 large egg
- 1 tsp vanilla extract
- 2 cups all-purpose flour
- 1 tsp baking soda
- 1/4 tsp salt
- 1/2 cup rainbow sprinkles

Instructions:

1. Preheat oven to 350°F (175°C).
2. Cream together butter, sugar, and brown sugar.
3. Add egg and vanilla extract, mixing well.
4. In a separate bowl, combine flour, baking soda, and salt. Gradually add to the wet mixture.
5. Stir in sprinkles.
6. Drop dough by spoonfuls onto a baking sheet.
7. Bake for 10-12 minutes.

Double Peanut Butter Cookies

Ingredients:

- 1 cup butter, softened
- 1 cup peanut butter
- 1 cup sugar
- 1 large egg
- 1 tsp vanilla extract
- 1 1/2 cups all-purpose flour
- 1 tsp baking soda
- 1/4 tsp salt
- 1/2 cup chocolate chips

Instructions:

1. Preheat oven to 350°F (175°C).
2. Cream together butter, peanut butter, and sugar.
3. Add egg and vanilla extract, mixing well.
4. In a separate bowl, combine flour, baking soda, and salt. Gradually add to the wet mixture.
5. Stir in chocolate chips.
6. Drop dough by spoonfuls onto a baking sheet.
7. Bake for 10-12 minutes.

Cashew Cookies

Ingredients:

- 1 cup butter, softened
- 1 cup sugar
- 1 large egg
- 1 tsp vanilla extract
- 2 cups all-purpose flour
- 1 tsp baking soda
- 1/2 tsp salt
- 1 cup chopped cashews

Instructions:

1. Preheat oven to 350°F (175°C).
2. Cream together butter and sugar.
3. Add egg and vanilla extract, mixing well.
4. In a separate bowl, combine flour, baking soda, and salt. Gradually add to the wet mixture.
5. Stir in chopped cashews.
6. Drop dough onto a baking sheet.
7. Bake for 10-12 minutes.

Carrot Cake Cookies

Ingredients:

- 1 cup butter, softened
- 3/4 cup brown sugar
- 1 large egg
- 1 tsp vanilla extract
- 2 cups all-purpose flour
- 1 tsp baking powder
- 1/2 tsp baking soda
- 1/2 tsp cinnamon
- 1/4 tsp nutmeg
- 1 1/2 cups grated carrots
- 1/2 cup chopped walnuts or raisins (optional)

Instructions:

1. Preheat oven to 350°F (175°C).
2. Cream together butter and brown sugar.
3. Add egg and vanilla extract, mixing well.
4. In a separate bowl, combine flour, baking powder, baking soda, cinnamon, and nutmeg. Gradually add to the wet mixture.
5. Stir in grated carrots and walnuts/raisins.
6. Drop dough onto a baking sheet.
7. Bake for 10-12 minutes.

Chocolate Dipped Biscotti

Ingredients:

- 1 1/2 cups all-purpose flour
- 1 cup sugar
- 1 tsp baking powder
- 1/4 tsp salt
- 2 large eggs
- 1 tsp vanilla extract
- 1/2 cup chocolate chips (for dipping)

Instructions:

1. Preheat oven to 350°F (175°C).
2. In a bowl, mix flour, sugar, baking powder, and salt.
3. In a separate bowl, whisk eggs and vanilla extract. Add to the dry ingredients and mix until a dough forms.
4. Divide dough into two logs and place on a baking sheet.
5. Bake for 20-25 minutes.
6. Let cool, then slice into 1/2-inch pieces.
7. Bake the slices for another 10-12 minutes to crisp.
8. Dip the biscotti into melted chocolate chips and let cool.

Poppy Seed Cookies

Ingredients:

- 1 cup butter, softened
- 1 cup sugar
- 1 large egg
- 1 tsp vanilla extract
- 2 cups all-purpose flour
- 2 tbsp poppy seeds
- 1 tsp baking powder
- 1/4 tsp salt

Instructions:

1. Preheat oven to 350°F (175°C).
2. Cream together butter and sugar.
3. Add egg and vanilla extract, mixing well.
4. In a separate bowl, combine flour, poppy seeds, baking powder, and salt. Gradually add to the wet mixture.
5. Drop dough by spoonfuls onto a baking sheet.
6. Bake for 10-12 minutes.

Maple Pecan Cookies

Ingredients:

- 1 cup butter, softened
- 1/2 cup brown sugar
- 1/4 cup maple syrup
- 1 large egg
- 1 tsp vanilla extract
- 2 cups all-purpose flour
- 1 tsp baking soda
- 1/4 tsp salt
- 1/2 cup chopped pecans

Instructions:

1. Preheat oven to 350°F (175°C).
2. Cream together butter, brown sugar, and maple syrup.
3. Add egg and vanilla extract, mixing well.
4. In a separate bowl, combine flour, baking soda, and salt. Gradually add to the wet mixture.
5. Stir in chopped pecans.
6. Drop dough onto a baking sheet.
7. Bake for 10-12 minutes.

Nutella Stuffed Cookies

Ingredients:

- 1 cup butter, softened
- 3/4 cup sugar
- 1/4 cup brown sugar
- 1 large egg
- 1 tsp vanilla extract
- 2 cups all-purpose flour
- 1 tsp baking soda
- 1/4 tsp salt
- Nutella (or other chocolate hazelnut spread) for stuffing

Instructions:

1. Preheat oven to 350°F (175°C).
2. Cream together butter, sugar, and brown sugar.
3. Add egg and vanilla extract, mixing well.
4. In a separate bowl, combine flour, baking soda, and salt. Gradually add to the wet mixture.
5. Roll dough into balls, make a well in the center, and fill with Nutella. Seal the dough around Nutella.
6. Bake for 10-12 minutes.

Cranberry White Chocolate Cookies

Ingredients:

- 1 cup butter, softened
- 3/4 cup sugar
- 1/2 cup brown sugar
- 1 large egg
- 1 tsp vanilla extract
- 2 cups all-purpose flour
- 1 tsp baking soda
- 1/4 tsp salt
- 1 cup dried cranberries
- 1 cup white chocolate chips

Instructions:

1. Preheat oven to 350°F (175°C).
2. Cream together butter, sugar, and brown sugar.
3. Add egg and vanilla extract, mixing well.
4. In a separate bowl, combine flour, baking soda, and salt. Gradually add to the wet mixture.
5. Stir in dried cranberries and white chocolate chips.
6. Drop dough by spoonfuls onto a baking sheet.
7. Bake for 10-12 minutes.

Chai Spice Cookies

Ingredients:

- 1 cup butter, softened
- 3/4 cup sugar
- 1/4 cup brown sugar
- 1 large egg
- 1 tsp vanilla extract
- 2 cups all-purpose flour
- 1 tsp baking soda
- 1/2 tsp ground cinnamon
- 1/2 tsp ground ginger
- 1/4 tsp ground cloves
- 1/4 tsp ground cardamom
- 1/4 tsp salt

Instructions:

1. Preheat oven to 350°F (175°C).
2. Cream together butter, sugar, and brown sugar.
3. Add egg and vanilla extract, mixing well.
4. In a separate bowl, combine flour, baking soda, cinnamon, ginger, cloves, cardamom, and salt. Gradually add to the wet mixture.
5. Drop dough by spoonfuls onto a baking sheet.
6. Bake for 10-12 minutes.

Banana Bread Cookies

Ingredients:

- 1 cup butter, softened
- 3/4 cup brown sugar
- 1 large egg
- 2 ripe bananas, mashed
- 1 tsp vanilla extract
- 2 cups all-purpose flour
- 1 tsp baking soda
- 1/4 tsp salt
- 1/2 tsp cinnamon
- 1/2 cup chopped walnuts or chocolate chips (optional)

Instructions:

1. Preheat oven to 350°F (175°C).
2. Cream together butter and brown sugar.
3. Add egg, mashed bananas, and vanilla extract, mixing well.
4. In a separate bowl, combine flour, baking soda, salt, and cinnamon. Gradually add to the wet mixture.
5. Stir in walnuts or chocolate chips, if using.
6. Drop dough by spoonfuls onto a baking sheet.
7. Bake for 10-12 minutes.

Pistachio Cookies

Ingredients:

- 1 cup butter, softened
- 3/4 cup sugar
- 1/4 cup brown sugar
- 1 large egg
- 1 tsp vanilla extract
- 2 cups all-purpose flour
- 1/2 tsp baking soda
- 1/4 tsp salt
- 1 cup shelled pistachios, chopped

Instructions:

1. Preheat oven to 350°F (175°C).
2. Cream together butter, sugar, and brown sugar.
3. Add egg and vanilla extract, mixing well.
4. In a separate bowl, combine flour, baking soda, and salt. Gradually add to the wet mixture.
5. Stir in chopped pistachios.
6. Drop dough by spoonfuls onto a baking sheet.
7. Bake for 10-12 minutes.

Chocolate Mint Cookies

Ingredients:

- 1 cup butter, softened
- 3/4 cup sugar
- 1/4 cup brown sugar
- 1 large egg
- 1 tsp peppermint extract
- 1 1/2 cups all-purpose flour
- 1/2 cup cocoa powder
- 1 tsp baking soda
- 1/4 tsp salt
- 1 cup chocolate chips

Instructions:

1. Preheat oven to 350°F (175°C).
2. Cream together butter, sugar, and brown sugar.
3. Add egg and peppermint extract, mixing well.
4. In a separate bowl, combine flour, cocoa powder, baking soda, and salt. Gradually add to the wet mixture.
5. Stir in chocolate chips.
6. Drop dough by spoonfuls onto a baking sheet.
7. Bake for 10-12 minutes.

Apple Cinnamon Cookies

Ingredients:

- 1 cup butter, softened
- 1 cup sugar
- 1 large egg
- 1 tsp vanilla extract
- 2 cups all-purpose flour
- 1 tsp baking soda
- 1/2 tsp ground cinnamon
- 1/4 tsp ground nutmeg
- 1/4 tsp salt
- 1/2 cup finely chopped dried apples or fresh apple chunks

Instructions:

1. Preheat oven to 350°F (175°C).
2. Cream together butter and sugar.
3. Add egg and vanilla extract, mixing well.
4. In a separate bowl, combine flour, baking soda, cinnamon, nutmeg, and salt. Gradually add to the wet mixture.
5. Stir in dried apples or apple chunks.
6. Drop dough by spoonfuls onto a baking sheet.
7. Bake for 10-12 minutes.

Chocolate Fudge Cookies

Ingredients:

- 1 cup butter, softened
- 1 cup sugar
- 1/4 cup brown sugar
- 1 large egg
- 2 tsp vanilla extract
- 1 1/2 cups all-purpose flour
- 1/2 cup cocoa powder
- 1 tsp baking soda
- 1/4 tsp salt
- 1 cup chocolate chips

Instructions:

1. Preheat oven to 350°F (175°C).
2. Cream together butter, sugar, and brown sugar.
3. Add egg and vanilla extract, mixing well.
4. In a separate bowl, combine flour, cocoa powder, baking soda, and salt. Gradually add to the wet mixture.
5. Stir in chocolate chips.
6. Drop dough by spoonfuls onto a baking sheet.
7. Bake for 10-12 minutes.

Cocoa Nib Cookies

Ingredients:

- 1 cup butter, softened
- 1 cup sugar
- 1/4 cup brown sugar
- 1 large egg
- 1 tsp vanilla extract
- 2 cups all-purpose flour
- 1 tsp baking soda
- 1/4 tsp salt
- 1/2 cup cocoa nibs

Instructions:

1. Preheat oven to 350°F (175°C).
2. Cream together butter, sugar, and brown sugar.
3. Add egg and vanilla extract, mixing well.
4. In a separate bowl, combine flour, baking soda, and salt. Gradually add to the wet mixture.
5. Stir in cocoa nibs.
6. Drop dough by spoonfuls onto a baking sheet.
7. Bake for 10-12 minutes.

Lemon Poppy Seed Cookies

Ingredients:

- 1 cup butter, softened
- 1 cup sugar
- 1 large egg
- 1 tsp vanilla extract
- 2 cups all-purpose flour
- 1 tsp baking soda
- 1/4 tsp salt
- 2 tbsp poppy seeds
- 2 tbsp lemon zest

Instructions:

1. Preheat oven to 350°F (175°C).
2. Cream together butter and sugar.
3. Add egg and vanilla extract, mixing well.
4. In a separate bowl, combine flour, baking soda, and salt. Gradually add to the wet mixture.
5. Stir in poppy seeds and lemon zest.
6. Drop dough by spoonfuls onto a baking sheet.
7. Bake for 10-12 minutes.

Cinnamon Sugar Cookies

Ingredients:

- 1 cup butter, softened
- 1 cup sugar
- 1 large egg
- 1 tsp vanilla extract
- 2 cups all-purpose flour
- 1 tsp baking soda
- 1/4 tsp salt
- 1/4 cup cinnamon sugar (for rolling)

Instructions:

1. Preheat oven to 350°F (175°C).
2. Cream together butter and sugar.
3. Add egg and vanilla extract, mixing well.
4. In a separate bowl, combine flour, baking soda, and salt. Gradually add to the wet mixture.
5. Roll dough into balls and roll in cinnamon sugar.
6. Place on a baking sheet.
7. Bake for 10-12 minutes.

Rocky Road Cookies

Ingredients:

- 1 cup butter, softened
- 3/4 cup sugar
- 1/4 cup brown sugar
- 1 large egg
- 1 tsp vanilla extract
- 2 cups all-purpose flour
- 1/2 cup cocoa powder
- 1 tsp baking soda
- 1/4 tsp salt
- 1 cup mini marshmallows
- 1/2 cup chopped nuts (optional)
- 1/2 cup chocolate chips

Instructions:

1. Preheat oven to 350°F (175°C).
2. Cream together butter, sugar, and brown sugar.
3. Add egg and vanilla extract, mixing well.
4. In a separate bowl, combine flour, cocoa powder, baking soda, and salt. Gradually add to the wet mixture.
5. Stir in mini marshmallows, chopped nuts, and chocolate chips.
6. Drop dough by spoonfuls onto a baking sheet.
7. Bake for 10-12 minutes.